The Untold Stories Of Women Driving
Innovation And Success From The Background

FEMALE LEADERS
BEHIND THE
SCENES

Only 8% of CEOs are women. Why is that? What
can we do to add more women to C-Suites?

Women Make Amazing Mentors

Women Handle Crisis Better

Women Are Better Communicators

Women Leaders Can Help
Bridge The Gender Pay Gap

Characteristics Such As Honesty,
Intelligence, Compassion, And Innovation
Rate Higher Among Women In C-Suites

Hanna Olivas And Adriana Luna Carlos
Along with 5 C-Suite Women Leaders

Table of Contents

INTRODUCTION

She Rises Studios was created and inspired by the mother-daughter duo Hanna Olivas and Adriana Luna Carlos. In the middle of 2020, when the world was at one of its most vulnerable times, we saw the need to embrace women globally by offering inspirational quotes, blogs, and articles. Then, in March of 2021, we launched our very own Women's Empowerment Podcast: *She Rises Studios Podcast*.

It is now one of the most sought out Women based podcasts both nationally and internationally. You can find us on your favorite podcast platforms, such as Spotify, Google Podcasts, Apple Podcasts, IHeartRadio, and much more! We didn't stop there. Establishing a safe space for women has become an even deeper need. Due to a global pandemic, women lost their businesses, employment, homes, finances, spouses, and more.

We decided to form the She Rises Studios Community Facebook Group. An environment strictly for women about women. Our focus in this group is to educate and celebrate women globally. To meet them exactly where they are on their journey.

It's a group of Ordinary Women Doing EXTRAordinary Things.

As we continued to grow our network, we saw a need to help shape the minds and influences of women struggling with insecurities, doubts, fears, etc. From this, we created a global movement known as:

Female Leaders Behind the Scenes

Behind every great success is a woman with conviction!

Female Leaders Behind the Scenes is a journey into the often unseen excellence responsible for many companies' success.

Navigating the terrain of female leadership from the shadows demands a unique blend of resilience, ingenuity, and determination. In a world where the spotlight often fails to reach those working tirelessly behind the scenes, this book stands as a beacon of recognition and empowerment.

Step into the realm of the uncelebrated, where the heartbeat of progress is driven by women who thrive in the background. Female Leaders Behind the Scenes offers an insightful exploration of the distinct challenges faced by these unsung heroines, while uncovering the invaluable wisdom they carry.

From cultivating an aura of professionalism that commands respect to refining leadership skills that whisper authority, this guide delves deep into the art of shaping impactful influence. With an emphasis on crafting a leadership style that's uniquely your own, you'll find inspiration to embrace your authentic voice while paving your own path to success.

As a female who is always behind the scenes, most of us don't get as much appreciation or celebration as one who is always in the spotlight. Yet, women continue to become a large part of everyday life in business and leadership.

She Rises Studios offers:

- She Rises Studios Publishing
- She Rises Studios Public Relations
- She Rises Studios Podcast (FREE to Listen to!)
- She Rises Studios Magazine
- Rise with Hanna Olivas - Featured on FENIX TV (FREE to watch!)
- She Rises Studios Community Facebook Page (FREE to Join!)
- She Rises Studios Academy

- KNOWN SRS
- FENIX TV (FREE to Watch!)

We won't stop encouraging women to be Unstoppable. This is just the beginning of our global movement.

She Rises, She Leads, She Lives...

With Love,

HANNA OLIVAS
ADRIANA LUNA CARLOS
SHE RISES STUDIOS
www.sherisesstudios.com

Adriana Luna Carlos

Founder and CEO of She Rises Studios & FENIX TV

https://www.linkedin.com/in/adriana-luna-carlos/
https://www.facebook.com/adrianalunacarlos
https://www.instagram.com/sherisesstudios/
https://www.sherisesstudios.com/
https://www.srslatina.com/
https://fenixtv.app/

Adriana Luna Carlos is an accomplished web and graphic designer, author, and mentor with a passion for helping women succeed in life and business. With over 10 years of experience in graphic and web arts, Adriana has built a reputation as an innovative leader and entrepreneur. In 2020, she co-founded She Rises Studios, a multi-digital media company and publishing house that has helped countless clients achieve their branding and marketing goals. In 2023, she co-created FENIX TV, an online streaming platform that showcases stories of people breaking barriers, shattering stereotypes, and triumphing against the odds.

As an advocate for women's success, Adriana challenges her clients and mentees to strive for nothing less than excellence. She has a deep understanding of the insecurities and challenges that women often face in the business world and provides the guidance and resources needed to overcome them. Her success as a business leader and entrepreneur has made her a sought-after mentor and speaker at events around the world.

Through her work, Adriana has demonstrated a commitment to creating opportunities for women to succeed in business and life. Her passion for innovation, leadership, and women's empowerment has made her a respected figure in the business community, and her impact will undoubtedly continue to inspire and empower women for years to come.

YOUR JOURNEY, YOUR SYMPHONY

By Adriana Luna Carlos

When we think about leadership, it's like remembering snapshots in a photo album – moments that stick with us and teach us important things. Looking back on my own journey, there are two stories that really stand out. These stories helped me understand what being a leader means and how I want to lead.

The first story takes me back to when I worked at a busy grocery store. There was this amazing manager who was totally different from the usual bosses. He didn't just tell us what to do; he worked alongside us. His attitude was incredible – always friendly and funny, making work enjoyable even when it was tough. He showed me that leadership is more than just giving orders; it's about working together and making everyone feel like they're part of a team.

Then there's another memory that's not so great. I used to work at a sign company, and my boss there was a bit of a micromanager. She would use cameras to watch everything we did, like she didn't trust us. I could hear the camera moving whenever I walked around the office. It was uncomfortable, and it made me realize that trust is a big part of good leadership.

Now, I don't just remember these stories for the memories. I use them to shape the way I lead. I treat my team with respect and try to understand their perspectives, just like that great manager did. And I avoid the micromanaging approach, focusing on trust instead.

As you think about your own journey, take a moment to remember instances where leadership played a role. Maybe it was during a school project where you guided a team to success or when you stepped up at a family event to keep things running smoothly. Think about how these moments shaped your understanding of leadership. Did they inspire you to collaborate more effectively, or did they ignite a desire to support others? Consider how these experiences continue to influence the way you manage people and situations today.

Our personal stories remind us that leadership isn't a one-size-fits-all concept. It's a blend of experiences, insights, and aspirations unique to each of us. As we explore the process of crafting our individual leadership styles, keep in mind that your journey, like mine, is woven with threads of growth, introspection, and a resolute commitment to inspire and make a positive impact.

Understanding Different Leadership Styles

Throughout my journey, I've come across a variety of leadership styles, each leaving its own mark on how I approach leadership. There's the "coach" style, where a leader guides and motivates their team, and the "visionary" who's always looking ahead and inspiring others. Then there's the "servant" leader, who prioritizes the needs of the team, and the "diplomatic" leader, skilled in handling different viewpoints. There are so many different styles to list and each style has influenced me in different ways.

For instance, observing a purely "coaching" leader made me appreciate the value of encouragement, but I also saw how it could limit adaptability. A "visionary" leader's enthusiasm is contagious, but it can sometimes overlook the nitty-gritty details. These lessons have shaped my own leadership style, which is a blend of these approaches. I adapt based on the situation—listening intently during team meetings to foster an open environment and then switching gears to hands-on support when it's time to execute tasks.

Embracing Your Authenticity

Embracing authenticity has been a key theme in my leadership journey.

When I think about the kind of leader I want to be, I'm reminded of those who left a positive impact on me. They were genuine and didn't shy away from showing their personality. They weren't afraid to be themselves, and that made the work environment more relatable and comfortable.

Drawing from this, I encourage my team to embrace their individuality. I want them to know that it's okay to be themselves at work. When you're authentic, it builds trust and makes others feel at ease. This doesn't mean being rigid—it's about staying true to your core values while being adaptable to different situations.

My experiences with various leadership styles have shown me the power of authenticity. It's not just a buzzword; it's a guiding principle that fosters a culture of respect, openness, and collaboration. By being authentic, you create a leadership style that's uniquely yours, and that's where the magic happens. Your team members will recognize and appreciate it, and they'll feel more motivated and connected. So, as we continue exploring the art of crafting a leadership style, remember that being yourself is the best way to inspire and lead others.

Being a Female Leader Behind the Scenes: Thriving in the Operations Role

Being a female leader behind the scenes isn't just a role I step into—it's where I genuinely come alive. While some people flourish in the spotlight, I've discovered that my true power and contributions shine brightest when I'm orchestrating things from behind the scenes.

What truly sets me apart as a leader is the sheer joy I find in being behind the curtain. There's an unmistakable sense of fulfillment and purpose that accompanies the meticulous work of ensuring everything runs like a well-oiled machine. I've always been drawn to the mechanics of an operation—the careful planning, the intricate coordination, and the precision of execution. While the stage is where the final act takes place, it's behind the scenes where the real magic is woven, piece by piece.

This preference for the operations side isn't just about comfort—it's about tapping into my strengths. I've come to realize that I'm at my best as a leader when I'm not in the limelight. It's not about avoiding attention; it's about embracing a role that lets me leverage my skills and expertise in the most impactful way. I've found that I can truly focus on the nitty-gritty details, anticipate potential roadblocks, and streamline processes when I'm not pulled in different directions by the demands of being in front of a camera or in the public eye.

What's truly intriguing is that this inclination towards leading behind the scenes doesn't dilute the impact of my leadership—it amplifies it. While my approach might not always command the same immediate attention as a charismatic leader in the spotlight, its influence is deeply felt in the results we achieve. The teams I've had the privilege of working with have experienced a remarkable sense of unity and purpose that emanates from a finely tuned operation.

Embracing Leadership: Your Journey, Your Symphony

Embracing your leadership journey and crafting your unique symphony involves a deliberate and introspective process. Let's break it down into actionable steps:

Step 1: Self-Reflection and Awareness

1. Explore Your Values: Take time to identify your core values and beliefs. What drives you? What do you stand for? Your values will serve as the foundation of your leadership style.
2. Assess Your Strengths: Recognize your strengths and areas where you excel. Are you a natural motivator, a strategic thinker, a problem solver, or a skilled communicator? Understanding your strengths will help you harness them in your leadership approach.

Step 2: Learn from Others

1. Study Different Styles: Familiarize yourself with various leadership styles, such as coaching, visionary, diplomatic, and servant leadership. Observe leaders you admire and identify elements you resonate with.

2. Extract Lessons: Reflect on the experiences you've had with different leadership styles. What worked well? What could be improved? Extract valuable lessons from both positive and negative encounters.

Step 3: Define Your Authentic Leadership

1. Embrace Your Authenticity: Understand that authenticity is your greatest asset. Embrace your true self, quirks and all. Authentic leaders are relatable and build stronger connections with their teams.

2. Identify Your Niche: Reflect on where you feel most empowered and effective. Do you shine as a mentor, a visionary, a mediator, or a hands-on supporter? Your niche is where your leadership truly comes alive.

Step 4: Cultivate Adaptive Leadership

1. Blend Styles: Combine elements of different leadership styles that resonate with you. Adapt your approach based on the situation—sometimes, a coaching style might be needed, while other times, a diplomatic approach might be more appropriate.

2. Effective Communication: Develop strong communication skills to convey your vision, expectations, and support to your team. Listen actively and create an open dialogue where ideas flow freely.

Step 5: Lead with Impact

1. Empower and Elevate: As a leader, your role is to empower your team, elevate their skills, and create an environment where they can thrive. Provide opportunities for growth and encourage their unique contributions.
2. Practice Trust and Transparency: Establish trust by being transparent about your intentions, decisions, and challenges. Trust is the cornerstone of strong leadership.
3. Continuous Learning: Commit to lifelong learning and growth. Seek feedback, attend workshops, read books, and learn from both successes and failures.

Step 6: Inspire Others

1. Share Your Journey: Share your leadership journey with your team. Be open about your experiences, challenges, and growth. Your authenticity will inspire others to embrace their own paths.
2. Encourage Individuality: Create an inclusive environment where team members feel safe to be themselves. Encourage them to embrace their strengths, ideas, and authentic selves.
3. Set the Tone: Lead by example. Your actions, attitude, and approach will set the tone for the entire team.

Step 7: Keep Striving

1. Set Ambitious Goals: Continuously challenge yourself and your team to set ambitious goals. Strive for excellence and encourage a culture of continuous improvement.
2. Celebrate Progress: Celebrate milestones and achievements along the way. Recognize and appreciate the hard work and dedication of your team.

Embracing your leadership journey and crafting your unique symphony is an ongoing process. It requires self-awareness, adaptability, and a genuine commitment to growth. As you step into your role as a leader, remember that your symphony is a work in progress—a masterpiece that reflects your values, experiences, and aspirations, and leaves a lasting impact on those you lead.

Hanna Olivas

Founder & CEO of She Rises Studios
Podcast & TV Host | Best Selling Author | Influential Speaker |
Blood Cancer Advocate | #BAUW Movement Creator

https://www.linkedin.com/company/she-rises-studios/
https://www.instagram.com/sherisesstudios
https://www.facebook.com/sherisesstudios
www.SheRisesStudios.com

Author, Speaker, and Founder. Hanna was born and raised in Las Vegas, Nevada, and has paved her way to becoming one of the most influential women of 2022. Hanna is the co-founder of She Rises Studios and the founder of the Brave & Beautiful Blood Cancer Foundation. Her journey started in 2017 when she was first diagnosed with Multiple Myeloma, an incurable blood cancer. Now more than ever, her focus is to empower other women to become leaders because The Future is Female. She is currently traveling and speaking publicly to women to educate them on entrepreneurship, leadership, and owning the female power within.

LEADING WITH HEART:
THE UNSEEN JOURNEY OF FEMALE LEADERS

By Hanna Olivas

Step into a world where leadership isn't just about the spotlight. In this chapter, I'm excited to pull back the curtain and show you the real behind-the-scenes of what it means to lead. As we journey together, you'll join me in tackling nerves, finding purpose in the chaos, and embracing the tools that make a difference. So, let's dive in and explore the heart of leadership—the stuff that doesn't always make the headlines but makes all the difference for you and your journey.

In the world of leadership, where the spotlight often shines bright, there's a different kind of magic that happens – the realm of female leaders who work tirelessly, often without applause, to create meaningful change. I invite you into the intimate space where I prepare for Rise episodes, embrace chaos with purpose, and learn to lead not just with authority, but with authenticity.

Embracing the Nerves: My Eminem Moment

Before the camera starts rolling and the interviews begin, I'll let you in on a little secret: nerves are part of the game. Even after all these years, interviewing celebrities can still make my heart race. So, how do I transform those jitters into unwavering confidence? I have my own personal anthem – "Lose Yourself" by Eminem. As those familiar beats thump in my ears, I feel a surge of energy and determination. It's like my nerves and excitement blend into this unique cocktail that fuels my conversations, making them real and unscripted.

Actionable Step:

Think about a situation where your nerves have held you back from taking the lead. What's your "anthem" that can transform those nerves into confidence? For example, whenever I feel anxious before a big presentation, I play [your chosen empowering song] and let its energy propel me forward.

Impromptu:

Imagine you're about to step into a nerve-wracking situation. What's your personal anthem? Fill in the blank with a song that inspires you, and describe how it empowers you to overcome your nervousness and step into your leadership role.

_____

_____

_____

_____

_____

The Beautiful Chaos of Purposeful Leadership

Picture this: a circus and a typhoon having a love child. That's what leading with a purpose looks like behind the scenes. It's not always tidy and predictable; it's a whirlwind of ideas, challenges, and a burning desire to make a difference. But within that chaos, there's an unmistakable sense of direction. We're not just leading for the sake of it; we're leading with a purpose that guides us through the storm, and somehow, we manage to make sense of the chaos and inspire others to join the journey.

Actionable Step:

Imagine your own unique metaphor for your leadership journey. What does it look like? For instance, my leadership journey is like a dance between a conductor orchestrating a symphony and a navigator steering through uncharted waters. This metaphor reminds me that purpose is the compass that keeps me on course.

Impromptu:

Create your own metaphor for your leadership journey. Fill in the blank with your chosen comparison, and explain how this metaphor resonates with your approach to purposeful leadership.

_____

_____

_____

_____

_____

The Toolbox of a Leader: Humor, Discipline, and Listening Ears

Leadership isn't just about giving orders and making big decisions. It's about cultivating a unique set of skills that often stay hidden behind the scenes. Imagine juggling humor that eases tension, discipline that fuels progress, problem-solving skills that dismantle barriers, and the art of listening that builds bridges. These are the tools that build the foundation of my leadership style, allowing me to connect, guide, and empower without needing a spotlight to do so.

Actionable Step:

Take a moment to reflect on your own leadership toolbox. What skills do you possess that might be hiding behind the scenes? How can you intentionally leverage these skills to create a more impactful leadership experience for yourself and those you lead? For instance, I've found that my ability to find humor in challenging situations has not only lightened the mood but also fostered stronger team bonds.

Impromptu:

Consider one specific skill from your leadership toolbox that you'd like to highlight. Fill in the blank with that skill, and share a real-life scenario where you successfully utilized this skill to overcome a leadership challenge.

_____

_____

_____

_____

_____

The Sacred "Holy Hour": Morning Rituals for Resilience

Let me take you into the heart of my mornings – a sacred time I call the "Holy Hour." Yep, I'm an early riser at 5 am, and that's not changing anytime soon. In this serene space, I gather my thoughts, set intentions, and mentally prepare for the day ahead. It's a ritual that helps me stay centered and focused, a secret ingredient that infuses my leadership with purpose and clarity.

Actionable Step:

Consider creating your own "Holy Hour" morning routine. What activities could you incorporate to set the tone for a purposeful day? Whether it's meditation, journaling, or exercise, carve out time for yourself each morning to set intentions and build resilience for the challenges ahead. For example, I start my day with a short meditation, followed by journaling my goals and affirmations. This ritual grounds me and primes me for a productive day.

Impromptu:

Craft your personalized "Holy Hour" routine. Fill in the blank with your chosen activities, and describe how this routine helps you approach your leadership role with clarity and resilience.

_____

_____

_____

_____

_____

Learning Across Borders: The Ever-Expanding Horizons of Leadership

Leadership isn't confined by borders; it's a journey that requires stepping outside our comfort zones and embracing different perspectives. Exploring other business cultures and welcoming diverse narratives is my way of staying in tune with the world. Growth is a constant, and through these experiences, I learn, evolve, and enhance my ability to lead with a deeper understanding and empathy.

Actionable Step:

Challenge yourself to learn from a business culture different from your own. This could involve reading books, attending seminars, or engaging with individuals from diverse backgrounds. How can you apply these learnings to enhance your leadership style and connect more authentically with your team? For instance, I recently attended a cross-cultural leadership workshop and discovered new approaches to team collaboration that I'm excited to implement.

Impromptu:

Imagine you're about to embark on a cross-cultural leadership journey. Fill in the blank with a specific culture you'd like to learn from, and describe how immersing yourself in that culture's values and practices could enhance your leadership effectiveness and empathy.

_____

_____

_____

_____

_____

As you've walked alongside me through the quieter moments of leadership, I hope you've discovered that true influence isn't always about standing in the limelight. It's about embracing nerves, channeling chaos, and nurturing a toolbox of skills that foster authentic connections. It's about those precious morning hours that set the tone for purposeful leadership and the unwavering commitment to continuous growth. Remember, even when the curtains fall and the applause fades, the heart and soul of leadership continue to thrive in the unseen, where passion and purpose intertwine.

Francine Juhlin

Founder of Personal Change Warriors LLC

https://www.facebook.com/PersonalChangeWarriors
https://personalchangewarriors.com/

Francine's thirst for adventure has shaped her remarkable and non-traditional journey of self-discovery. She departed from her parents' home and embarked on an exhilarating adventure in the Navy. Francine fearlessly joined the world's largest boys' club, defying gender norms in pursuit of adventure. Despite not always being accepted as a leader, Francine demonstrated her leadership skills from behind the scenes, setting an inspiring example for others to follow. Her passion for the military didn't wane after leaving the Navy. Instead, Francine was drawn to the Army National Guard and found herself in Iraq during Operation Iraqi Freedom. After watching her fellow male noncommissioned officers lead and fail, Francine came out from behind the scenes to lead. Taking the road less traveled, Francine added a "female" touch to leadership, breaking barriers, and defying stereotypes. Francine's leadership, though unconventional for the Military, proved to be effective and inspiring to subordinates and seniors.

WOMEN BEHIND THE SCENES

By Francine Juhlin

THE ROAD LESS TRAVELED

I never meant to be a leader. My actions were all in pursuit of knowledge and adventure. For many years, I did nothing more than work hard and fight for my right to be who I wanted to be as I figured out what exactly that was. Although I still don't know what I want to be when I grow up, I know that wherever the road less traveled takes me, it will surprise even me. I also did not take a traditional route to leadership. I emerged from the background as a non-traditional leader.

Being a serial runaway made me feel like I was failing in life. As I learned and grew, I kept running away. I ran away from my childhood home. I ran away from the Navy. I ran away from my first marriage. I ran away from my authentic self. Later in life, I realized I wasn't running away from anything, but running to something better. I ran to new experiences. I ran to education. I ran to safety. I ran back to myself. I ran to success.

After graduating from high school and starting college, something was missing in my life. At 17 years old, I was a high school graduate, college student, and the head cashier at a hardware store. Being both a full-time student and a full-time worker was difficult. I felt no sense of adventure and excitement. I felt no sense of upward mobility. After one semester, I decided that I needed something more in my life. The road less traveled led me to self-discovery in the pursuit of what was missing.

I was not looking for easier. I was looking for more. I didn't know what more was, but I wanted it. I had friends in the Navy, and it looked like they were having fun. They were earning money and learning a trade. I wanted that. I needed adventure while figuring out what I wanted to be when I grew up.

Looking back more than 40 years, I realized I often felt like something was missing. Most of the time, I was missing self-esteem, self-confidence, and safety. Although I had a steady stream of achievements, I kept searching for something to make me feel accepted and secure. I also searched for excitement and adventure. I had to find what was missing.

My need for adventure led me on a non-traditional path of discovery. I discovered that I am a resourceful and strong person. I discovered that my feeling of lack drove me to new experiences and challenges. This discovery came from a journey of winding roads and exciting circumstances. The road less traveled allowed me to find parts of myself I would never have found if I followed a traditional route to adulthood.

On February 14, 1983, I left my parent's home in the suburbs of Chicago and started my journey as a sailor. I remember seeing my mom cry as the recruiter and I left our driveway. Although I felt bad that I made my mom cry, I was excited about the dawning of my big adventure.

In the Navy, I learned marketable skills. In the Navy, I learned that hard work pays off. In the Navy, I learned how to be one of the guys to fit in. I ran away from my femininity as a coping mechanism for my membership in the biggest boy's club in the world. In the Navy, I learned that the most important leadership I needed to exhibit was leading myself.

LEAD BY EXAMPLE

My education as a young sailor reinforced the knowledge that hard work would get me what I wanted. I grew up in a family that considered hard work essential to living, so I felt confident I could deliver. I also learned that taking the path less traveled requires even more hard work. I had to work to be accepted before I could work to achieve.

When I joined the Navy at 18 years old, I went in as a non-designated striker. The Striker program allowed me to learn about the different jobs available and choose the one best suited for me. Several times, leaders of the squadron tried to talk me into joining the administrative team. I did not know what I wanted to be, but I did know that I did not want to be a secretary. As I attempted to find a permanent job, I learned that men did not want women in their male-dominated field of aircraft maintenance. It would have been far easier for me to take a "female role" and fit into the environment. I always steered toward the non-traditional path, which always requires me to work hard for what I want.

Because I never felt like I fit in as a child, I usually chose the path less traveled, hoping I would find where I belonged. It's possible that I made some choices in an attempt to say, "Hello, I'm here. Does anyone want to claim me?" My lifelong journey attempting to fit in gave me the ability to cross cultural lines. This discovery helped me understand that the road less traveled allows me to fit in anywhere.

When choosing a musical instrument in grammar school, I did not choose a standard "female" instrument. Most girls in the fifth grade chose the flute, clarinet, or saxophone. I chose the tuba. I always told the story that I chose the tuba because we could borrow the instrument from the school, so my parents did not have to buy me an expensive instrument. I really chose the tuba because I always sought attention. A 5'2" little girl carrying a tuba into a concert always attracted attention.

My work ethic kept me on task. The tuba was not a difficult instrument to learn, but it was hard to handle the large brass mass because I was not an athletic kid. I mastered playing the tuba by the time I started high school, and the natural progression was to join the marching band. The other tuba players had a hazing ritual. The new "guy," or

13-year-old girl, had to carry the brass sousaphone. A brass sousaphone weighs about 35 pounds. The guys carried the 15-pound fiberglass sousaphones. I had strong legs by the end of marching season. They thought I would not make it through the year, but I worked hard.

This work ethic kept me on task while finding my vocation in the Navy. I worked support duties in the organization. I learned how to service aircraft and guide the pilots to the parking spots. I led an effort in the tool room to establish a new inventory system. I excelled at every task given to me, completing it on time with zero defects. The one task I could not complete was finding a work group to accept me as an apprentice. Then I met Marty, a work center supervisor, who recognized my work ethic.

Marty took me under his wing and taught me to be an aircraft electrician. This was a win/win situation. As I learned, I worked hard to learn more. I worked eight hours in my support duties, then worked an additional eight hours in the aircraft electrical shop. My days off were extended study sessions. Marty taught me about Ohm's Law, aircraft lighting, wiring, and other areas of Naval Aviation I needed to know to pass the exam to become an official aircraft electrician, in lieu of going to a primary trade school. Marty used me as an example to motivate the men who took for granted that they did not have to struggle for acceptance into their boy's club. My hard work motivated my coworkers. Marty's tutoring helped me pass the exam to become an aircraft electrician, which I was for more than 30 years.

After ten years in the Navy, I let my ex-husband persuade me to become a civilian again. I ran away from the Navy with him to Yazoo City, Mississippi. This was a time of learning and education for me. Coming from Chicago, the back woods of Mississippi were a major culture shock. In retrospect, Mississippi and living with my southern in-laws were more shocking than Navy basic training.

I should have run away from him much earlier, but I finally came to my senses and ran away in the middle of the night to protect myself from a serial abuser. It was time to lead myself to a new life. After getting the abuser and his girlfriend out of the house I was paying for and getting my car back from them, I ran away from the house that carried the memories of a failed marriage.

I made some bad decisions to have a "safe place" to sleep. I felt like my safety could be in jeopardy at any time. I retreated within while sitting at a four-way stop on the road less traveled. I hid from everything but my job. Hard work kept me focused on something other than my lack of safety and stability.

My desire for safety led to a right turn at that four-way stop where I was parked. At first, I felt that my failed marriage meant I was a failure. During this vulnerable time, I learned that I'm resourceful and strong. However, the abuser's words kept fear in my heart. The words from my abuser were the catalyst for learning how to protect myself physically. He constantly told me that if I ever left him, he would hunt me down and kill me, so I joined the Army National Guard to learn self-defense and how to fire a weapon.

I found the Army a new and exciting experience. However, I was still in the biggest boy's club in the world. I was also in the Mississippi National Guard and had to navigate southern attitudes. To say that the men didn't consider me an equal would be an understatement. I was not a leader in the Army because, although I was an aircraft electrician, I was new to the Army experience. Eventually, the time came that I flexed my leadership muscles in the Army. I led myself to advocate for work opportunities.

The story I'm about to tell you happened in Iraq in 2004, about six months into our one-year deployment. I watched my fellow male noncommissioned officers lead and fail as a Electrical/Avionics Branch squad leader. Based on seniority, I should have been among the first to be assigned a leadership role.

I spent my first few months in Iraq organizing our spare parts, turning in broken equipment, and supporting the men while they did the "important work." Eventually, I started doing aircraft maintenance when nobody was looking. I was a shift supervisor when I was in the Navy; my full-time job before and after Iraq was as an aircraft electrician; I was one of the most experienced electricians in our section. But the leadership in my Mississippi National Guard Unit could not see past the fact that I was a girl.

After several discussions with the Platoon Leader and Maintenance Officer, I wore them down. I was finally given an opportunity to be the squad leader on a trial basis. They essentially gave me a trial period to prove I could do the job I did years earlier while in the Navy.

The first threat to my success during my leadership trial began when our squad of seven was shorthanded. One man was on leave. One man was on guard duty. One man was sick in quarters. When arriving for our night shift, I was met at the door with a red-faced Sgt French yelling that he was on strike because they did not get his pay right in six months. For those of you who do not have military experience, the military is not represented by a union. Therefore, we had no right to strike. My first dilemma had a whole lot of moving parts that needed to all go in the same direction while trying to satisfy everyone involved.

I listened to Frenchie's story and understood his frustration and anger completely. He was not receiving his dependent's pay and fell behind on his child support. My test as a leader was to ensure my crew's needs were met while ensuring the electrical systems were working properly on all the aircraft required for the flights. Although I empathized with Frenchie, he did not make my job easy.

I reported to the maintenance officer that we had a challenge for the evening. The maintenance officer was ready to teach me how to do discipline paperwork since Sergeant French refused to work. I decided to take a more nurturing approach and allow Frenchie to feel his feelings for the evening. I had to muster all the gentle and kind leadership instincts I possessed to explain to the two workers who showed up for work that we had to pick up the slack of our coworker on strike.

I cannot write the words I heard after explaining that Frenchie would not work and that we had to complete our list of tasks without his help. My road less traveled changed the tone for the rest of the evening. After ample time to voice their opinions, I asked a question. I thought there would be a confrontation, but my defiance of the standard military protocol was met with understanding. I achieved buy-in by simply asking a question.

My feeling of compassion led me to approach the Sergeant-on-strike situation differently than my male counterparts would have. My question was, "How would you feel if you had a choice between paying your mortgage or your child support?" The question was met with silence. Then, I could see understanding and compassion on their faces.

My small team and I completed the work necessary for our helicopters to go on their missions for the evening. Frenchie had his time to "lick his wounds." By taking the road less traveled and showing compassion and understanding, we brought more attention to Frenchie's dilemma, and his pay problems were addressed. Instead of adding insult to injury and filing disciplinary paperwork, we found a solution for the payment problems and saved the career of a talented worker. The road less traveled led my coworkers to a new understanding of teamwork.

My road to leadership took many turns and detours. Sometimes it felt like I was running away. Looking back, I realize I was running to new adventures and working toward my next chapter. I never felt like I fit in. Looking back, I realize I fit in everywhere I was meant to be. In the pursuit of knowledge and adventure, I emerged from the background as a non-traditional leader leading by example and with compassion.

Richelle Pena

Co-Founder of American Pediatric Dental Group

http://linkedin.com/in/richellepena
https://www.facebook.com/thelifestyleleader
https://www.instagram.com/richellepena_/
www.RichellePena.com

Richelle Pena was born and raised in Miami, Florida. After finishing school to become a pharmacist, she found a different calling. Together, with her husband, Richelle founded the American Pediatric Dental Group. They built their brand over the course of a decade, expanding to seven locations spread across South Florida before being acquired by a larger dental organization in 2021. The experience formed one of the greatest moments of her life to date and inspired her to detail her journey in the hopes of inspiring others to follow their dreams.

Richelle is the mother of three beautiful children. Together as a family, they love traveling and exploring the world. She has visited over 50 countries and uses her joy of food to immerse in the different cultures in ways few can accomplish. Eternally positive and brimming with energy, Richelle has found purpose in self-care, attributing her individual growth to being able to love and care for others. Passionate about leadership, Richelle seeks to help women unlock and achieve the elusive work-life balance. In her spare time, she enjoys running and taking pure barre classes. Being a wife, mother, and entrepreneur is a demanding yet rewarding experience and is the foundation for her latest project.

Follow Richelle @richellepena_
Website: www.RichellePena.com

HOW BEING "JUST A PHARMACIST" PROPELLED ME INTO LEADERSHIP AND ENTREPRENEURSHIP.

By Richelle Pena

"Don't be like us, be better than us."
—Ricardo Garcia

I am a second-generation Filipino American, born in Miami, FL, on May 23, 1982. My parents, Teresita and Ricardo Garcia, are both from the Philippines and moved to Miami in the 1970s on work visas to fulfill the lack of nurses in the United States. Like many immigrants, they came to the US in search of a better future. Growing up, my parents always made sure we had dinner together as a family at the end of a long day. This was the time when we would talk about our day and when my dad preached about how we should not be like them, but be better than them. He said this with so much conviction because he saw all the opportunities we had in the United States to become successful.

If I was going to be better than them, then I knew I didn't want to be a nurse. Filipino parents always encourage their kids to become nurses because it is a "safe and stable" career. I have a lot of respect for nurses, but I just didn't want to be another Filipino nurse. My parents are not your typical Filipino parents who usually just want to play it safe. They lived outside their comfort zone, which indirectly instilled confidence in me at an early age. I admired how they came to the US with no family and no money yet worked their way up to later becoming entrepreneurs through hard work. I knew I could accomplish anything in life as long as I had determination, dedication, and worked hard.

I still decided to pursue a career in the medical field because I knew it was "safe" and something that would always be in need. However, it wasn't going to be nursing. I was accepted into the accelerated pharmacy program to get my Doctor of Pharmacy degree. This was a stable job that paid well upon graduating, and it was a step above a bachelor's degree. Did I love pharmacy? No. But, the "Asian" mentality of having a good education and a respectable career was all I knew, so I decided to become a pharmacist.

How becoming a pharmacist ignited my love for leadership and business.

I graduated in 2007 from pharmacy school. I didn't realize that being "just a pharmacist" would propel me to learn business and how to be a leader. After all, I spent four years learning about the chemical properties of drugs, their mechanisms of action, and their adverse effects. I was a pharmacy intern at Target Pharmacy for a few months until I passed the California pharmacy law exam. I was flagged as a "high potential" manager at Target during my internship. A high potential at Target is someone with the ability, engagement, and aspiration to rise to and succeed in more senior, critical positions. I went from being an intern to a pharmacy manager position in Pinole, California as soon as I got my license to practice. Although I was scared, I accepted the challenge. For the first time in my life, I had to learn financials and lead a team. I didn't have any business training in college, but I was equipped with the confidence and can-do attitude my parents instilled in me growing up. I saw my parents grow from being nurses (employees at a hospital) to becoming entrepreneurs and owning their own nursing agency. Therefore, I like to say that entrepreneurship runs in my blood.

Thankfully I was not pushed into the deep end and was taught valuable tools during a two-week intensive "business college." This experience opened my eyes to the world of business and leadership. They had courses on team culture, systems and processes, compliance, human resource (interviewing, hiring, and firing), and store financials. I was given the opportunity to be part of the pharmacy operations team. I learned essential business skills such as pharmacy acquisitions, interviewing pharmacists, and pharmacy interns, supporting low-performing stores, and meeting with regional leaders. I became so passionate about the business part of pharmacy that I wanted to be relieved of my mundane pharmacy duties, such as filling prescriptions and dealing with insurance. Although I loved talking to my patients and building relationships, I knew I had a gift to lead and motivate a team. One of the best skills I built as a pharmacist was to be a good listener and be empathetic.

Moving back to Florida.

While I was working at Target in California, my fiancé and now husband, William Pena, was completing his advanced training in pediatric dentistry residency. Will and I wanted to start a family, so we decided to move back to Florida, where we met and grew up. He had a vision of opening dental offices for underserved children and patients with special needs, but he lacked the business acumen and asked me to join him in his new venture. Around the same time, we decided to open our first pediatric dental office together, my first child, Adrian Pena, was born on June 22, 2011. I embraced the challenges of being a new mom, sleepless nights, and caring for someone other than myself. My life changed forever.

Turning point in my career.

A quote repeated often by Will: "Dream big and shoot for the moon. Even if you miss, you will land among the stars."

Since I had the corporate knowledge from being a pharmacist at Target, he knew I would be the best business partner to make our business a success! I was excited to create a business centered around building a positive team culture and always doing what is right for the patient.

Learning is a lifelong endeavor.

I didn't fully understand what I was getting myself into when I decided to work alongside my husband. Up until this point, we both had separate careers and would not bring work home, meaning our dinner conversations were not around work 24/7. We both knew that opening a business from the ground up would take sacrifice.

American Pediatric Dental Group opened its doors on Nov. 11, 2011. We were a team of five people, an office manager, two dental assistants, Will, and myself. I worked at the front desk alongside the office manager to learn all the administrative tasks of running a dental office. I learned everything from billing to insurance. I also answered the phones and learned how to schedule patients. If we were going to scale this to many locations, I knew we needed documented systems and processes. My hands-on experience helped us create processes that could be replicated in each new office. This also made sure there were no "sacred" cows who were indispensable. Since customer service and building a positive team culture was an area where I excelled, I knew that we needed the right team members working for us.

Aside from learning the day-to-day administrative operations, I was the marketing manager. Before opening the business, I liaised with a website designer to create our website and logo. I also managed our social media on Facebook and our Google business page. We were living in an era where office reviews were crucial to your success. I had no prior marketing experience. You can learn anything if you have the willingness to put in the work. I knew that marketing was the only way people would know about our office. Eventually, word of mouth would be our number one referral.

A company must have a strong purpose.

It was important from day one that we had a strong purpose and mission statement. Having a business with a strong purpose leads to a more engaged team and loyal customers. Our business aimed to treat the underserved children in the community. When we opened our first office, there were more than a dozen pediatric dentists within a five mile radius. But we were different. Not only did we have a brand-new state-of-the-art office, but we also accepted most major dental insurance plans, including state Medicaid. There were not many pediatric dentists willing to see patients on state insurance because the reimbursement was so low. We focused on creating memorable and "wow" experiences one patient at a time. I ensured our team was hyper-focused on providing excellent customer service and going above and beyond for our patients. It was also important that we were accessible to working parents, so we opened late evenings and Saturdays. Our company was a major disruptor in the dental field because most dentists only wanted to work 9-5pm and no weekends.

Once you find your niche and how to be different from your competitors, go all in and be the best in your market!

Dream Big

We had just celebrated our grand opening in January 2012 with a full-blown party. If you think big and act upon it, you will attract it to your life. I wanted the community to know we were here and ready to make a splash. I hired the best radio station to play music at our grand opening and announce our new dental office, had an elaborate ribbon cutting with the Mayor of Pembroke Pines, and invited all the dentists in the area to celebrate. We decided to name our company American Pediatric Dental Group, a grandiose name, for only being a small practice with only one doctor at the time because our vision was to have offices in many communities. On the night of the grand opening, someone commented: "Who is the group? Are there other doctors working here?" We chuckled and answered, "No, but one day we shall have many offices."

That same night, I found out I would be pregnant with my baby girl, Leia Pena. I was so nervous because Adrian was only six months old and had a brand-new business. That year, I would learn how to juggle being a mom, wife, and entrepreneur without sacrificing my own self-care.

At work, Will was the CEO. At home, I was the Chief Home Officer "CHO."

In 2014, we were blessed with another baby girl, Annabelle Pena, into our family. Not only did I have three kids under the age of three years old, we also expanded our operations and opened two more locations. Rather than acquiring existing dental offices, we decided to build each office from the ground up. We pursued this route because we wanted each office to be replicated in every city with the same look and feel. In addition, we didn't want to inherit teams that may not jive with our team culture. We were still considered a small business but needed more team members to sustain our growing operations. Not only did our team triple in size, but so did our expenses.

Will and I both have alpha personality types with a strong sense of leadership, determination, and ambition. I knew if we wanted to work together and stay married, we had to divide and conquer. I took the lead in the areas where I excelled, such as building relationships with the community, marketing, leading the call center, and building a positive team culture. He took the lead with the financials and led the clinical operations.

I am the Chief Home Officer "CHO" and leader at home. I take care of our social calendar, including all the family events, playdates, and travel plans. I also love to cook and have dinner together as a family every night. Quality time with my family and strong faith in God are more important to me than anything else in the world.

Crucial conversations and working with your significant other.

Working with your husband or significant other is not easy. We knew that having open and honest communication was imperative, even if it was uncomfortable. The most difficult conversations that always put a knot in my stomach were those around finances, both at work and at home. I knew that God put it in our hearts to build a business around helping children, which gave me faith and hope in the future of our organization.

I will never forget one of the most crucial conversations Will and I had one night in 2016. We were running out of money to sustain our large overhead. My heart sank because a large team relied on us, plus three young kids at home. We would have this conversation again several times after that year, but in 2019 it got real. We had six locations and were in negotiations on our first dental acquisition. It was a dentist that was selling his practice to have a better quality of life. By 2020, we had seven locations.

We needed to do more with less to sustain our operations and be profitable. Within a year, we had to lay off three directors and outsource the call center and insurance department to save money.

Knowing when to exit.

I love seeing a business grow. It was a challenge for me to fill the offices with patients every time we opened a new location. In 2019, we opened a satellite office to test the market before opening an office in that city. We were only open two to three days a week, and I struggled to fill the schedule. I deployed the same marketing strategies I did for our other offices, but I was hitting a dead end. I started to see a shift in the dental business and realized we were no longer unique. Pediatric dental offices were opening in every corner and copying our business model. Just like us, these offices accepted all dental insurance plans, opened late evenings and weekends, and were modern and state-of-the-art.

After the corporate restructuring to save money, we were finally profitable after almost ten years in business! We accomplished something that everyone thought we were crazy for doing- serving the underserved and building a business around a strong purpose.

After ten years of being in business, my husband and I grew American Pediatric Dental Group to seven locations in South Florida with over 130 team members, 18 doctors, and serving over 50,000 patients. In 2021, we were acquired by a DSO (dental service organization).

Balance

So how did I do it all and not lose myself? I prioritize self-care, self-love, and personal growth with mindfulness and self-reflection, and honoring my needs.

Now, as a devoted mother of three, I understand the delicate art of balancing family life and personal aspirations. My mission is to help women unlock the secrets of work-life balance. My latest project, The Lifestyle Leader, provides me with the opportunity to guide women as they step into their power and create lives they truly love, inspiring them to embrace their full potential and cultivate a life of balance, authenticity, and boundless possibilities.

Carrie Wehunt

Coach

https://www.facebook.com/profile.php?id=100002340907098

My name is Carrie Sokolowski Wehunt. I am the mother of three beautiful children: Dalton, Hayden Claire, and Grayson. I have been a teacher for 24 years in first grade, science, library, PE, and sign language. During my career as a teacher, I coached many sports for middle and high school students, along with the Battle of the Books teams. I played three sports at Juniata College and was inducted into the Sports Hall of Fame in October 2014 for Softball, Field Hockey, and Women's basketball. I was a trainer for years, empowering women to become stronger mentally and physically so they could enjoy their lives to the fullest. I have a background in sports conditioning for varsity sports and different ages of kids. I love spending time with my kids, coaching, assisting, and cheering them on. I owe all my accomplishments and life achievements to God, my family, and my friends.

PLAY TO LEAD

By Carrie Wehunt

Ever since I was a little girl, I've been in love with the concept of sports. It didn't matter what type of sport or who was playing it, I couldn't get enough of the excitement, competition, and pure joy that comes with watching a sports game—from the adult softball games at the neighborhood park to the pick-up basketball games at the community pool, the swim meets at the neighborhood pool, the local high school games, and of course gymnastics on TV.

When I reached the age where I could start participating in sports, I wanted to try everything—gymnastics, ballet, basketball, soccer, T-ball, swimming, etc. I looked forward to every practice and anxiously awaited game days. My parents realized early on that nothing else mattered to me except my sports. I didn't care about my hair, clothes, make-up, boys, or even talking on the phone like every other kid in the 80s and 90s. As long as I was laughing with my teammates, sweating from playing hard, practicing to become better, and strategizing on how to win, I was happy.

Just like life, sports has its ups and downs, pros and cons, moments of pure bliss and moments of complete failures. I embraced the failures in my sports because they provided opportunities to become better, stronger, and more determined. Some of the greatest athletes have experienced failures in their sports careers. Michael Jordan said, "I failed over and over in my life, and that's why I succeeded. Failure gave me strength." Success creates automatic feelings of joy and happiness—feeling like you're on top of the world, but failure can create two types of feelings—feelings of bitter anger, which leads to giving up, or a feeling of determination which leads to an opportunity for success. Mindset and attitude create the stepping stones for joy and happiness, which I learned in my years of playing sports.

Early Years in Sports

My father was my basketball coach through middle school. Not sure if it's what he always wanted to do, but the opportunity presented itself, and he stepped in with uncertainty, excitement, and determination. Working with middle school girls is no easy task. He often had to set rules about "hair, makeup, boys, and girl drama." When we came to practice, it was time to focus on basketball—becoming a team, learning from our mistakes, and pushing forward to become better. My father often referred to analogies of the greatest moments in sports history: "The name on the front of your jersey is more important than the one on the back. Win, lose, or tie, you're going to play like champions," spoken by the late Herb Brooks. My dad has always modeled for me the kind of athlete, teacher, parent, teammate, coach, and leader I wanted to be.

During these years, there were many wins and moments of greatness in championships, playoffs, and tournaments, along with moments of complete losses, overtime defeats, pure blow-outs, and utter embarrassment. Within all of these experiences and moments, I couldn't get enough of the game. I was taught from a very young age to never quit, never give up, and that if you want it badly enough, you go after it—you figure it out no matter what. So within each game and with each passing year, I grew not only as a player but as a leader on and off the court. I found my purpose within sports. I encouraged my teammates to keep going, work harder, smile and enjoy the moments, to become stronger, but most importantly, to always love the game.

High school brought more opportunities to be involved in multiple sports at a higher level of play. But with those opportunities came many challenges. As a freshman, I played on the JV basketball team with all my teammates that had been coached by my father. We did not play on the freshman team because we were well-experienced players in the game. In some aspects, we were a force to be reckoned with—many wins and lots of blow-outs. When the season was over, many of us transitioned into softball, another sport I could not get enough of—the rush of playing third base, stealing bases for the win, hitting home runs and line drives to advance my team, and mastering left-handed 'slap bunts.' We carried over our intensity, drive, determination, and athleticism from basketball champs to softball champs. Our class of girls quickly became known for being incredible athletes with tons to accomplish.

Moving into our sophomore year of high school, we were being recruited by the Varsity Head Basketball Coach. This coach was known for being aggressive and verbally intense in her coaching style. Some would even say "emotionally abusive" in her demands and expectations on and off the court. Many of my teammates decided to stay on JV where they were comfortable and enjoyed the coach as well as the 50-point leads and blow-outs. After much reflection during the fall, I made the personal decision to step up and play Varsity. I knew I needed to be challenged and pushed to improve if I ever wanted to pursue basketball in college. It was hard to leave my teammates, but it was something I needed to do, so I never looked back or regretted passing up an opportunity for growth. About halfway into the season, the pure exhaustion and feeling of defeat had set in, and I was slowly beginning to doubt myself. I doubted my ability to play, my ability to overcome challenges, my ability to "get up" when knocked down, but most importantly, I doubted my ability to lead. I was struggling and losing myself and losing the love of the game. My family, especially my father, spent many days and nights processing all my feelings, emotions, doubts, and fears with me. I was always taught never to fear anyone but playing for a coach who tore me down as an athlete instead of building me up to be the best I could be made me realize it was time to step away from the game and take a break. If I didn't, I most likely would never play ball again. I realized I had nothing to prove to anyone, especially myself. I hung up my basketball shoes and knew when the time was right, I would put those shoes back on and lead once again on the court. Until then, I was going to channel my energy, time, and passion into other sports.

As I entered my junior year, my English teacher was also the girls' Varsity field hockey coach. She was incredibly tenacious about getting me to try out the sport. Every day she asked, and every day I declined. Until the day she said to me, "What do you have to lose? If you don't like it, don't play; but if you do like it, I guarantee you will learn to love it." I was intrigued and made the commitment to show up at a practice. The stick was placed in my hand, and the rules were explained. This sport was so foreign from the sports I had played growing up. Quickly I realized field hockey was hard and challenging, a sport that frustrated me throughout the practice. I couldn't believe how much I was challenged physically and mentally in this sport. At the end of practice, my coach came to me and said, "Well? What did you think?" I looked at her with confusion, frustration, and exhaustion and said, "I'll see you tomorrow," and got in my car and left. Each day I showed up more determined to learn the game and to play it to the best of my ability. I became captain and led my team to several wins in my junior and senior years. I was hooked and fell in love with the sport. Field hockey was not the only challenge I faced in my later years of high school. My softball season senior year impacted me tremendously. Halfway through my senior season and halfway into a game, my catcher blew her knee. It was a time of uncertainty and desperation for our coaches because "Who was going to finish the game?" As I stood next to third base, my assistant coach, for whom I had an incredible amount of admiration as a teacher and coach, said, "Carrie is our catcher." What? I looked at him and shook my head no, to which he responded, "You are an athlete that can do whatever you put your mind to. Go and put on the gear!" As I looked around and saw everyone staring and waiting for a response, I took a deep breath and walked over to start putting on the catcher gear. I walked silently behind the plate, squatted down in a catcher's position, raised my glove, and said, "I'm ready!" My pitcher smiled with a sense of relief but also uncertainty. I reassured her that we got this and began shouting field directions to my teammates. Several batters had either gotten simple hits or struck out until a runner on first decided to steal second. Without hesitation I gunned the ball as hard and fast as I could right into my shortstop's glove, getting the third out in the inning. My teammates were shocked and speechless, and my coach said, "Welcome to your new position for the rest of the season." I knew at that moment it was another opportunity to grow and lead, so I smiled and said, "You got it!"

Later Years in Sports

My college years were filled with more moments, challenges, and opportunities in sports. While deciding where I wanted to attend school, I was being heavily recruited by the field hockey coach for Juniata College. She had heard about my story, reviewed my stats, and had several conversations with my high school coach. Jill La Point knew she wanted me as a part of her team, so she called relentlessly, asking for me to come and visit the campus and team. I had declined her offer multiple times until one day, my father accepted her offer. This was a moment when my father was not in my good graces. He kept reassuring me I needed to look into every opportunity and never "judge a book by its cover." We sat in silence the entire ride to the visit, and I kept silent as I was introduced to the coach and a few of the girls on the team. My silence encompassed multiple feelings—frustration, disappointment, anger, and disinterest, but I smiled and followed. I was immediately introduced to the rest of the team, brought to an off-season practice, and taken out to meet and experience the "campus life." Upon pick up the next day, my dad looked at me and said,

"Well?" I smiled and said, "I'm home." Within a few days of the visit, I submitted my application and was accepted and given a spot on the field hockey and softball teams. The practices were hard, the seasons were fun, and the memories were indescribable. During my years at Juniata, I was captain of the field hockey and softball teams, acquired incredible stats, and made friendships that would last a lifetime.

When I wasn't in season with either sport, I always played pickup basketball games with random players and friends. I didn't own a pair of basketball shoes because I never intended to return to the game. But after watching me play ball for several years, the women's basketball coach asked me to be a walk on my senior year. I laughed and said, "I don't play anymore. The time has passed." She disagreed and asked me to join a practice. Once again, I found myself in a situation of "What do I have to lose?" I jumped into a few of the pre-season practices and slowly found myself falling in love with the game all over again as if I had never left. I accepted the offer to play and became a senior captain and starter. By the time I was getting ready to graduate from college, I had been a four-year player/captain for field hockey and softball and one year captain for basketball. At the awards banquet, I received the Bargerstock Award—senior female athlete who made the greatest contributions to Juniata athletics. I was humbled. I never had an expectation to receive any recognition for playing sports. To me, it was always about loving the game.

After I graduated, I returned home to my high school, where I took a teaching job and coached multiple sports. I coached field hockey for my former high school and coached basketball and softball for National Cathedral School for Girls in DC. I left teaching high school to pursue my degree in elementary education and taught first grade. I continued to coach high school sports for several years until I turned my focus to coaching middle school sports. I wanted to coach younger students and develop athletes before they got to the high school level.

During my years of coaching middle school sports, I coached girls' and boys' basketball, baseball, and softball and started a field hockey program. I always knew I wanted to impact and encourage young kids to stay active and play sports. I wanted them to love sports. From all my years as a player, I knew from all the ups and downs, successes and failures, and challenges, what kind of coach I wanted to be: a coach that LEADS. When it was time to have children, I stepped out of the teaching and coaching world because I wanted to raise my kids while never missing a moment. When my kids got to the age of playing sports, I jumped into every opportunity I could to coach and assist them—swim team mom, acrofitness mom, soccer mom, softball mom, basketball mom, volleyball mom, cross country mom, field hockey mom, and ice hockey mom. I instilled the love of the game into my kids as well as their friends and teammates.

About nine years ago, my kids witnessed one of the greatest moments in my life: my induction to the Sports Hall of Fame for Juniata College. It was the most intimidating, exciting, and humbling experience I have ever been blessed with. The idea of giving a speech and receiving an award of recognition for my sports was overwhelming, to say the least. What was I going to say? Where do I begin? As always, my family, especially my father, encouraged me to speak from the heart. "Tell them your story," he said. For 20 minutes, I told my story—from my earliest memory I was in love with sports—from the challenges, the friendships, the mountains to climb, and the "love of the game." I spoke about how my life experiences had provided me with the tools to become a female leader in and out of the classroom as a teacher, a female leader on and off the courts and fields, and a female leader in my children's eyes.

I have a Hall of Fame plaque at Juniata College. I recently took my kids to visit the campus, meet the administrators and coaches, and walk down memory lane with them. As my kids read my plaque, tears filled my eyes:

"A three-sport athlete, Sokolowski (maiden name) was a recipient of the Charles Bargerstock Award; presented to the senior female athlete who made the greatest contributions to Juniata athletics. She had a .336 career batting average as an all conference shortstop and ranks in the Juniata top 10 all time in batting average, triples, and homeruns. Sokolowski finished her field hockey career with 14 goals, five assists, and 33 career points. She joined the basketball team her senior year and played in 19 games, finishing the season with 28 rebounds, 16 points, 15 steals, and 12 assists."

They weren't tears of sadness but tears of pure joy and happiness. Through all my failures and challenges, I was able to lead with integrity, honor, and grace, accomplishing more than I ever dreamed possible. But none of it was possible without the support of my family, friends, coaches, and most importantly GOD. I am proud of my accomplishments, but I'm more proud that every decision I made and every path I chose led me to become the empowering leader I am today as a mother, friend, trainer, teacher, daughter, sister, and coach.

When my students, my athletes, and my children ask me: How did you become a leader? Here are my thoughts:

"Great moments are born from great opportunity."
— Herb Brooks

"How you play today, from this moment, is how you will be remembered. This is your opportunity to rise and grab glory."
— Jack Lengyel (Marshall University)

"Be brave—take the hill. But first ask yourself, 'What's your hill?'"
— Matthew McConaughey

"Sometimes all you need is 20 seconds of courage."

"You have to be obsessed with whatever your win is. Be all in."
— Kobe Bryant

"When you fail, your feelings give you excuses. Your mind makes you more resilient." — Tim Grover

"What is your WHY? When you have an opportunity, why would you give 80%? Always give 120%" — Eric Thomas

Whatever your WHY is, do it with the opportunity to lead. NEVER forget those that supported and encouraged along the way, and NEVER forget to thank God. For with Him everything is possible.

Dr. Heidi Gregory-Mina

CEO of Dr. Heidi Business Psychologist

https://www.linkedin.com/in/dr-heidi-gregory-mina-47b140b7/
https://www.facebook.com/drheidigregorymina/
https://www.instagram.com/dr.heidi_/
www.drheidigregorymina.com
www.chroniclesofcrazyhazelnut.com

Dr. Heidi Gregory-Mina is a highly regarded business psychologist, esteemed professor, and accomplished author known for her ability to combine research and practical applications. Drawing on her real-world experience, she offers insights into human behavior, empowering clients and readers to enhance their performance. Through workshops, seminars, consulting, and speaking engagements, Dr. Heidi helps individuals and organizations achieve their objectives. As the host of the "Dr. Heidi The Business Psychologist" podcast, she shares her expertise with a broad audience, exploring topics like business psychology, leadership, and personal development. With over 20 years of nonprofit experience before entering higher education, Dr. Heidi brings a unique perspective. She values education and community engagement as catalysts for positive change, reflecting her diverse background and dedication to social responsibility.

SILENT BATTLES, VICTORIOUS STRIDES

By Dr. Heidi Gregory-Mina

I am the President of the second-largest company in the world. I started as a data entry clerk twenty years ago and slowly worked up to finally become President two years ago. Actually, none of that is true, but wouldn't it be nice? Many of our male counterparts have inspiring success stories that follow a clear and smooth trajectory, starting from humble beginnings and culminating in powerful leadership positions. However, for women, the path to success is often marked by numerous obstacles and a lack of equal opportunities. The disparity between male and female achievements in the corporate world is a stark reminder of the work that still needs to be done to achieve true gender equality.

Like many women, I have navigated a diverse career path to advance in my professional journey. It wasn't until I made the decision to venture out on my own that I had the opportunity to showcase my leadership skills. When I speak of shining as a leader, I don't necessarily mean being in the limelight, as effective leadership often involves empowering others to take the lead. However, I have yearned for recognition of my accomplishments, fair compensation, and equal chances for advancement. These aspirations reflect the desire that many women have to be acknowledged and rewarded based on merit, regardless of gender.

The Early Days

During the early stage of my career, I had a remarkable opportunity to interview for a leadership position. Throughout the process, I felt a genuine alignment between my skills and the requirements of the job. As I progressed to the final round of interviews, I grew confident that I would be offered the position. However, the weekend passed without the anticipated call, and instead, I received a note informing me they had chosen another candidate. The news left me bewildered and cast doubt on my instincts, prompting a cascade of questions and introspection.

Several months later, I had an unexpected encounter with the hiring manager. As we started talking, we delved into the topic of the leadership position I had interviewed for earlier. To my surprise, she divulged the true reason behind their decision: my age (i.e., childbearing age) and the potential for maternity leave. Her statement stirred a mix of emotions within me. On one hand, there was a sense of relief, as it validated my initial intuition and suspicions. On the other hand, a deep sense of dismay settled in, as I realized that despite the progress society has made, issues of gender inequality still exist. The realization served as a reminder of the hurdles women face in their careers and the persistent biases that hinder advancement.

So, how does one move forward? Turning disappointment into fuel for growth, I refused to allow the information from the hiring manager to become a defining moment in my career. Instead, it ignited a fire within me, fueling determination to prove my worth and challenge biases that hindered my progress. This can be done by seeking out opportunities for growth, building a strong support network of mentors and allies, advocating for yourself and others, and continuously learning and developing new skills. Additionally, it is important to confront and address any systemic barriers or biases that may exist within your organization or industry, and to actively promote gender equality and inclusivity.

The Move to Healthcare

As I continued to look for a position, I stumbled across a job in the healthcare sector. I was called for an interview and found the position interesting. This felt like a good next step, and shortly after the interview, I was offered the position. Knowing that the healthcare industry is considered primarily feminine, I did not anticipate gender barriers. However, I was naive.

I immediately questioned whether I was purposely misled during the interview or if it was ignorance. I began hearing stories about high turnover in the department, specifically within this position. I started to wonder if they were searching for a scapegoat when they hired me. Companies often place women in these precarious positions—a phenomenon referred to as the glass cliff, where women are more likely to be appointed to leadership positions in challenging or precarious situations, where the risk of failure is high.

Despite the initial alignment between the job description and my skills, I soon realized the extent of my inadequacy in meeting the demands of the role. With limited internal training available, I embarked on a rigorous journey of self-improvement, dedicating years to acquiring the necessary knowledge and skills. Through determination and a commitment to personal growth, I transformed from a novice to an expert in my field, overcoming obstacles and emerging with a deep sense of accomplishment and resilience.

Kept to the Sidelines

As I delved into my job, I continued to encounter challenges that tested my resolve. Questioning internal processes within the organization became inevitable as I observed discrepancies in how I was being treated compared to my colleagues. It perplexed me why I, despite being the one actively contributing and driving results, was excluded from key meetings with the Department Chair. Seeking clarity, I expressed my concerns to my boss, only to be met with dismissiveness and a lack of satisfactory explanation.

This experience reinforced the need to confront biases and advocate for fairness, pushing me to seek opportunities where my contributions would be recognized and valued. As I reflect back, I realize that I should have spoken up and demanded answers. If that did not work, I should have taken my complaint to HR. However, like many other women, I did not want to rock the boat for fear of retaliation.

One day, while on my way to lunch, I happened to run into the Department Chair, and we engaged in small talk. Eventually, the conversation turned to his research grants, and he asked me to relay questions to my boss. Instead, I answered his questions right then and there. He appeared surprised. As we continued to talk, it became clear that the work I had been doing was being attributed to my manager; I was receiving no credit for my contributions. It was in that moment that I realized I could no longer tolerate such a hierarchical culture.

I made the decision to embark on a new chapter by pursuing a doctorate degree and transitioning into higher education. I felt that having a higher degree would open new doors and add credibility to my background. Leveraging the flexibility of my position, I strategically balanced my responsibilities while working diligently towards my goals. The day I handed in my resignation I was met with shock from my manager, who had been oblivious and believed he had a strong hold on me, assuming I would never leave. This moment of departure symbolized my liberation from a toxic environment and marked the beginning of a journey where I would chart my own path and define my own success.

The Move to Higher Education

Transitioning into higher education, research, and consulting opened doors for me. Higher Education is built on learning, professional development, and individual growth, so I did not believe I would encounter biases. Again, this was naive, and I now realize no industry is immune to these issues, and as women leaders, we need to know how to recognize the signs.

I seized the opportunity to step into my first teaching position, specializing in Management Information Systems (MIS). Gratitude filled my heart as I realized that many teaching positions were often filled based on personal connections. As doubts began to creep in after the interview, I couldn't help but notice that I didn't quite fit the typical dynamics of the other instructors. Despite these uncertainties, I remained confident in my knowledge and teaching abilities, determined to carve my own path in academia.

I recall coming home and expressing my thoughts, saying, "I think I got this position because I am a younger, blonde female." This realization deeply affected me. When I went for training, I met with the department head. As I entered his office, he closed the door and said to me, "We are so happy to have you. We got rid of one old fogey and gained one young chicky." Hearing those words and having them validate my suspicions was gut-wrenching. I didn't feel like I could continue working within that group, but I had made a commitment to the students. Therefore, I taught my class, gathered my course reviews, and ultimately found a way to transfer to another department. I did not want a position because I was a *young woman* but rather because I was the most qualified.

Breaking Through with a Mentor

As I transitioned, I had the incredible fortune of finding a mentor who played a pivotal role in shaping my success. Throughout history, many women have become successful with the help of their support structure and mentorship. One example is Indra Nooyi, the former CEO of PepsiCo. During her tenure, she was mentored by the former CEO, Roger Enrico. Enrico played a significant role in shaping Nooyi's leadership style and providing guidance as she navigated her way to the top. He not only supported her professional development but also encouraged her to take risks and step out of her comfort zone. Under

Enrico's mentorship, Nooyi was able to develop her strategic thinking, decision-making abilities, and business acumen, ultimately leading her to become one of the most influential women in the corporate world. Their mentor-mentee relationship demonstrates the value and impact of mentorship in fostering the growth and success of female leaders. So, one way women leaders break through is having a mentor. But how do you get a mentor? Attend networking events, ask questions, set up times for coffee chats, and use social media groups. Mentors give you a support system, guide you through decisions, and support you when circumstances are out of your control.

My mentor's support and guidance was instrumental in my journey. Through his mentorship, I gained invaluable insights into the significance of audience engagement, nurturing creativity within the classroom, and finding innovative approaches to challenge and inspire my students. The impact of his teachings was evident as my classes became highly sought after, with waitlists growing longer each semester. The recognition I received for my distinctive class activities further affirmed the profound influence of my mentor's guidance. To this day, I am grateful for the opportunity to continue working closely with my mentor, who has evolved into a trusted friend and colleague.

Cultural Hesitancy

Women tend to check out of their career development as soon as they decide they are going to have children; this is often referred to as the maternal wall. We stop looking for promotions, turn down assignments, and much more for fear of job loss or being further dismissed in the workplace. Many women hesitate to reveal they are pregnant and wait for as long as possible. While this may seem like a barrier that cannot be overcome, gaining individual awareness and engaging in self-reflection will help us make more conscious decisions. Additionally, we should look at all of our options and build in diversification so we can remain agile leaders.

Despite not experiencing any additional direct discrimination in my teaching endeavors, I still felt reserved and hesitant to disclose my pregnancy. I worried that it could negatively impact my career and future teaching opportunities. As a result, I worked until my due date and returned immediately after the holidays. When people eventually found out about my daughter, they expressed disbelief. They reassured me that I should have informed them, as they would have been supportive and there would have been nothing to worry about.

Despite my accomplishments and expertise, I have noticed a decline in the number of course opportunities offered to me since becoming a mother. I also received comments suggesting that I should be spared additional responsibilities due to having a toddler. While these comments may stem from well-intentioned concern, I believe the decision to balance work and family should be mine to make, not predetermined by others. This situation served as a catalyst for me to begin asserting my own path and focusing on my consulting work. Diversification and having other options will allow for stability for myself and family. Embracing this new direction, I ventured into speaking engagements, conducting workshops, authoring books, and launching my own podcast. This journey has allowed me to explore my true self on a deeper level and provide me with the opportunity to connect with individuals, companies, and nonprofits, sharing my knowledge and expertise in a meaningful way. It is through this pursuit that I strive to inspire and empower others, particularly women, to embrace their own unique paths and achieve success while maintaining a healthy work-life balance.

Fear is Good

The onset of the pandemic brought about significant changes in the way education was delivered. It was during this transformative time, coupled with personal milestones such as the birth of my daughter and closing a side business, that I began reflecting deeply on my aspirations. I realized that there was a greater potential for me to make a lasting impact and contribute more meaningfully. However, there was one obstacle standing in my way: my fear of failure. These invisible barriers hold women back in their careers. Invisible barriers are subtle obstacles or biases that hinder progress or limit opportunities for certain individuals or groups, often without being readily apparent or explicitly acknowledged. For myself, it is all about taking the first step. I found that once I get started and overcome what I refer to as the "first three," everything begins to go smoothly. It can be three minutes, three seconds, three people, three obstacles, but that gut-wrenching feeling of fear always disappears at this number.

The experience of closing a business we had worked tirelessly to grow over five years heightened this fear. Despite grappling with uncertainty, I spent a year contemplating the idea of expanding beyond the classroom to share my knowledge with a larger audience and focusing on growing my consultancy. Eventually, I summoned the courage to take the leap. This endeavor demanded that I put myself front and center, as the success of the business relied solely on me. As an introvert, venturing into this new territory pushed me far beyond my comfort zone. I slowly began to realize that **FEAR IS GOOD**! It means that something important is happening, and stepping out of our comfort zone is the only place where growth happens.

In conclusion, my journey through various professional challenges has shed light on the obstacles that women face in their careers and the need for continued efforts to achieve gender equality. While my story may not align with the typical success narratives, it highlights the systemic biases and obstacles that hinder women's progress. The disparity between male and female achievements underscores the pressing need for gender equality and equal opportunities. Despite encountering numerous setbacks and facing limited recognition for my accomplishments, I have remained steadfast in my pursuit of success. Take the first step, embrace personal growth, seek out mentorship, challenge societal norms, and advocate for fairness and inclusivity. Through my own journey, I strive to inspire and empower other women to break free from limitations, pursue their aspirations, and make their mark in their respective fields. Together, we can create a more equitable and inclusive world where women are acknowledged, valued, and given equal opportunities to thrive and lead.

Cheri Dixon

Cheri Dixon Consulting
Coach

https://www.facebook.com/cheri.dixon.35
https://www.instagram.com/cheridixonconsulting/
www.findagirlandherdog.com

Cheri Dixon is the owner of Cheri Dixon Consulting and an elementary principal. She always knew she was going to have an impact on the world, which started with teaching children so that they could grow up with options in their lives. Cheri found that she wanted to shift her career and help women live their best lives. After going through many ups and downs in her own life, she found that she could help women build a life they love with the right support system by their side. Cheri is a co-author of the book Unleash Her, published through She Rises Studios. Her newest course focuses on middle-aged women who have lost themselves in their everyday lives and want to become the unstoppable woman they knew they were born to be! Cheri's first talk show, Confident, Courageous, and Clear, is on Fenix TV!

LEAD, SERVE, LOVE

By Cheri Dixon

I never thought I would become a leader in the world of education. I knew I wanted to teach children, but leading was not on my radar. As they say, leaders are born, and someone saw the leadership skills in me early in my teaching career. I became an elementary principal at a fairly young age for a female leader. Although I continue to be the face of the schools I lead, my leadership style is to serve my community, my students, and my staff. I am only as strong as they are and that is what has helped me successfully lead three schools over the past 16 years and feel confident that I have what it takes to be a valued and trusted leader.

I used to watch leaders from all different backgrounds, professions, and cultures. I would see that the leader was usually a very charismatic, confident person who had the ability to get others to see and follow their vision. I would also see how the most successful would put their people's needs first, giving of their time, energy, and focus to ensure everyone who follows them can do so at their own highest level. You see, being a leader is being about people. Of course, we need management skills: organization, time management, monitoring… things that need to get done need to get done. But a successful leader balances this with soft skills: building others' confidence, listening when someone has a problem, problem-solving situations in a way that puts the organization first, and most importantly communicating with their followers with the utmost respect in all situations.

Wikipedia defines leadership as, "the ability to lead, influence or guide others." Furthermore, great female leaders are described as, 'vulnerable, authentic, humble, transformative, bold, risk-takers, empathetic, and kind.' You see, those that lead well continue to use people skills that serve not only their own people but lift others in ways that exude respect, value, and trust.

I find that there are three guiding principles that I continuously prioritize. The first is leading to all. I would never expect anyone in my community to do anything that I would not attempt to do myself. I must always be the example in all situations and I hold myself to a very high standard when it comes to my integrity, work ethic, and support of my people. If leading means influencing or guiding others, I do this by believing in them, motivating them, and pushing them to their own highest level while modeling my own dedication and desire to do my very best in all situations, even when no one is watching. I find that others will work for leaders who believe in their skills and support them when they need extra help, acquire new skills, or just that gentle nudge in the right direction.

My second principle is to serve. Leadership is not about accolades or awards. Leadership is not about being told you are doing a great job. Successful leadership is about the success of those that I lead. And I can only do that when I am at service to them in a way that lets them know that they are on the front lines, doing the hard work, with me standing strong alongside them to provide whatever they need. For example, my teachers work directly with my students. I need to build their skills and believe that they will, in turn, use their skills to deliver instruction to the students in a way that moves them forward academically. If I have a teacher who doesn't understand how to deliver a lesson or use a specific strategy, I step in and assist in a way that teaches the teacher how to deliver effectively, while not losing a minute of learning with our students. This support not only gives them real-time learning opportunities, but I also follow up by then observing the teacher using the same process and providing feedback to help them continue on a path of success. For me, this not only serves my teacher at the highest level, but I also continue to keep myself on that "front line" so that I never forget the stress and high-level intensity of teaching children each day. I have never had a teacher decline this support or provide me with feedback that this was not a helpful way to build their capacity. I know they also appreciate the fact that I keep grounded in the real world of teaching in the classroom.

I could not do this work or lead at my highest level if I did not have the love needed for the profession and the work my community does. Love is my third guiding principle, and to be honest, it may be the most important of them all. I believe that you can easily walk into a school building and feel the love of all who work there. It is communicated by how they interact and show up each day. This is the whole premise of climate and culture, and it matters. If this part of your world as a leader is not there, you will struggle. Your followers and your community need to know you care, you would be there for them no matter the circumstances, and that you love them in a way that they can feel comfortable working and taking chances to learn, grow, and thrive. I know my staff, I know all my students, and I know the needs of my community. This helps me lead, serve, and love each one and has contributed to the success of each community I have led and ultimately, my own success as a leader.

Leadership includes those managerial skills, but true leadership, the kind that is going to make your organization the best place it can be, balances those skills with the best soft skills in a way that allows everyone to thrive and do their very best work!

JOIN THE MOVEMENT!
#BAUW

Becoming An Unstoppable Woman
With She Rises Studios

She Rises Studios was founded by Hanna Olivas and Adriana Luna Carlos, the mother-daughter duo, in mid-2020 as they saw a need to help empower women around the world. They are the podcast hosts of the *She Rises Studios Podcast* as well as Amazon best-selling authors and motivational speakers who travel the world. Hanna and Adriana are the movement creators of #BAUW - Becoming An Unstoppable Woman: The movement has been created to universally impact women of all ages, at whatever stage of life, to overcome insecurities, and adversities, and develop an unstoppable mindset. She Rises Studios educates, celebrates, and empowers women globally.

We Are
SHE RISES STUDIOS
A real-life community of women working to become the best version of themselves to change their lives and make the world a better place.

LEARN MORE

Looking to Join Us in our Next Anthology or Publish YOUR Own?

She Rises Studios Publishing offers full-service publishing, marketing, book tour, and campaign services. For more information, contact info@sherisesstudios.com

We are always looking for women who want to share their stories and expertise and feature their businesses on our podcasts, in our books, and in our magazines.

SEE WHAT WE DO

OUR PODCAST   **OUR BOOKS**   **OUR SERVICES**

  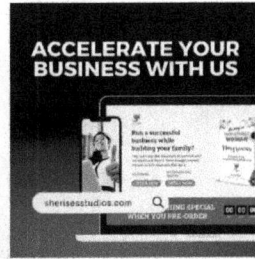

Be featured in the Becoming An Unstoppable Woman magazine, published in 13 countries and sold in all major retailers. Get the visibility you need to LEVEL UP in your business!

Have your own TV show streamed across major platforms like Roku TV, Amazon Fire Stick, Apple TV and more!

Learn to leverage your expertise. Build your online presence and grow your audience with Fenix TV.
https://fenixtv.sherisesstudios.com/

Visit www.SheRisesStudios.com to see how YOU can join the #BAUW movement and help your community to achieve the UNSTOPPABLE mindset.

Have you checked out the *She Rises Studios Podcast?*

Find us on all MAJOR platforms: Spotify, IHeartRadio, Apple Podcasts, Google Podcasts, etc.

Looking to become a sponsor or build a partnership?

Email us at info@sherisesstudios.com

SHE RISES
STUDIOS

www.ingramcontent.com/pod-product-compliance
Lightning Source LLC
Chambersburg PA
CBHW060257030426
42335CB00014B/1747